HOW CAN I CULTIVATE
PRIVATE PRAYER?

✘ CULTIVATING BIBLICAL GODLINESS

Series Editors
Joel R. Beeke and Ryan M. McGraw

Dr. D. Martyn Lloyd-Jones once said that what the church needs to do most of all is "to begin herself to live the Christian life. If she did that, men and women would be crowding into our buildings. They would say, 'What is the secret of this?'" As Christians, one of our greatest needs is for the Spirit of God to cultivate biblical godliness in us in order to put the beauty of Christ on display through us, all to the glory of the triune God. With this goal in mind, this series of booklets treats matters vital to Christian experience at a basic level. Each booklet addresses a specific question in order to inform the mind, warm the affections, and transform the whole person by the Spirit's grace, so that the church may adorn the doctrine of God our Savior in all things.

HOW CAN I CULTIVATE
PRIVATE PRAYER?

JOEL R. BEEKE

REFORMATION HERITAGE BOOKS
GRAND RAPIDS, MICHIGAN

How Can I Cultivate Private Prayer?
© 2016 by Joel R. Beeke

Reformation Heritage Books
2965 Leonard St. NE
Grand Rapids, MI 49525
616-977-0889
orders@heritagebooks.org
www.heritagebooks.org

Printed in the United States of America
18 19 20 21 22 23/10 9 8 7 6 5 4 3 2

ISBN 978-1-60178-455-1

For additional Reformed literature, request a free book list from Reformation Heritage Books at the above regular or e-mail address.

HOW CAN I CULTIVATE
PRIVATE PRAYER?

The gospel produces a praying people.[1] Christ died to bring us to God (1 Peter 3:18). God calls sinners into union with Christ by the gospel (1 Cor. 1:9) so that in Christ we can have fellowship with Him (1 John 1:3). God has forged in Christ an unbreakable link between the human needs of His people and His infinite resources.[2] Yet it is not God's will that those resources flow to us without our hearts being engaged. God sends His Spirit into the hearts of His children so that they cry out in prayer to the Father (Rom. 8:15; Gal. 4:6). Indeed, they not only cry out *to*

1. Portions of this booklet are adapted from Joel R. Beeke, "Prayerful Praying Today," in *Taking Hold of God: Reformed and Puritan Perspectives on Prayer*, ed. Joel R. Beeke and Brian G. Najapfour (Grand Rapids: Reformation Heritage Books, 2011), 223–40. Thanks to Paul Smalley for his assistance.

2. John Calvin, *Institutes of the Christian Religion*, ed. John T. McNeill, trans. Ford Lewis Battles (Philadelphia: Westminster Press, 1960), 3.20.1.

God (Ps. 57:2) but they also cry out *for* God (Ps. 84:2). He is their greatest desire (Ps. 73:25).

Christian prayer is a holy communication between the believing soul and heaven, a spiritual exchange of the desires and praises of God's children for the blessings of their Father in heaven. The Westminster Shorter Catechism expresses it well: "Prayer is an offering up of our desires unto God (Ps. 62:8), for things agreeable to his will (1 John 5:14), in the name of Christ (John 16:23), with confession of our sins (Ps. 32:5–6; Dan. 9:4), and thankful acknowledgment of his mercies (Phil. 4:6)."[3] John Bunyan echoed that definition effectively: "Prayer is a sincere, sensible, affectionate pouring out of the heart or soul to God, through Christ, in the strength and assistance of the Holy Spirit, for such things as God has promised, or according to His Word for the good of the church, with submission in faith to the will of God."[4]

Prayer is a crucial part of the Christian life and deserves our careful attention and cultivation. Praying is as natural to true Christians as breathing is to a living child. When God's people pray, they breathe forth the living motions of their faith, repentance, submission, obedience, hope, and love.

---

3. Westminster Shorter Catechism, Q. 98, in *Reformed Confessions of the 16th and 17th Centuries in English Translation: 1523–1693*, ed. James T. Dennison Jr. (Grand Rapids: Reformation Heritage Books, 2014), 4:367.

4. John Bunyan, *Prayer* (repr., Edinburgh: Banner of Truth, 1965), 13.

However, just as a child needs to grow, so believers in Christ need to grow in their praying. Indeed, a child's breathing can be dangerously hindered by illness, and at times the prayer life of a believer can be constricted and enervated by spiritual diseases. Therefore, we do well to examine ourselves and emulate the disciples, who said, "Lord, teach us to pray" (Luke 11:1). Felicity Houghton writes, "Prayer is the way by which Christians express and develop the relationship that God Himself has chosen to make with them as their Father through Jesus Christ.... As often as I pray, I still find I need to be taught how to pray."[5]

TAKE INVENTORY OF YOUR PRAYER LIFE

James 5:17 says that the prophet Elijah "prayed earnestly." Literally, the text says that Elijah "prayed in his prayer" (KJV marginal note 1). James is using a Hebrew idiom intended to intensify the force of the verb. In other words, Elijah's prayers were more than a formal exercise; he was pouring himself into his praying. Alexander Ross observes, "A man may pray with his lips and yet not pray with an intense desire of the soul."[6] You might call it "prayerful praying."

---

5. Felicity B. Houghton, "Personal Experience of Prayer I," in *Teach Us to Pray*, ed. D. A. Carson (London: World Evangelical Fellowship, 1990), 300.

6. Alexander Ross, *The Epistles of James and John*, The New International Commentary on the New Testament (Grand Rapids: Eerdmans, 1954), 102.

Consider the tremendous potential of prayer. It is nothing less than communion with the living God. Thomas Brooks wrote, "Ah! How often, Christians, hath God kissed you at the beginning of prayer, and spoke peace to you in the midst of prayer, and filled you with joy and assurance, upon the close of prayer!"[7]

The great possibilities of prayer should awaken us to the meager realities of our own praying. Is prayer the means by which we storm the gates of heaven and take the kingdom by force? Is it a missile that crushes satanic powers, or is it like a harmless toy that Satan sleeps beside? Are we more concerned about what our human listeners think of our words than about our communion with God? How often do we truly experience prayerful passion for the presence of God?

Our prayer life may be "closed for repairs," though little repair work seems to get done. Good intentions surface from time to time, but wishes and intentions are no substitute for repentance and the persevering implementation of better habits. The problem is that when our prayer life is boarded up, everything else begins to shut down. How can we live to God in public when we so seldom meet Him in private? Prayerless praying begins to cool long before reaching heaven and falls back on us as cold

---

7. *The Works of Thomas Brooks*, ed. Alexander B. Grosart (1861–1867; repr., Edinburgh: Banner of Truth, 2001), 2:369.

rain to chill the soul, while prayerful praying lifts us into the light of heaven and warms the soul. Thomas Adam frankly admitted, "I pray faintly, and with reserve, merely to quiet conscience, for present ease, almost wishing not to be heard…. Prayer and other spiritual exercises are often a weariness to me."[8] Is that the condition of your prayer life?

As Greg Nichols points out, a prayerless person is *ungrateful* because he does not thank God, *self-righteous* because he does not confess his sins to God, *self-centered* because he does not ask God to bless other people, *presumptuous* because he does not pray even for his daily needs, *irreverent* because he does not praise God nor pray for His kingdom to come, and *unfriendly to God* because his prayerlessness evidences that he does not enjoy being with God.[9] If your heart is absolutely prayerless, then you are not a child of God. Your first step toward cultivating a prayer life is the step from death to life. You must repent of your sins and trust in Christ alone for salvation.

What then of the true believer who has a praying heart but finds himself stumbling in his prayers? How can he improve? He must take hold of himself and take hold of God.

---

8. Thomas Adam, *Private Thoughts on Religion* (Glasgow: Chalmers and Collins, 1824), 68, 73, 76.

9. Greg Nichols, "Prayerlessness" (Grand Rapids: Truth for Eternity Ministries, n.d.), tapes GN-E 1–4.

TAKE HOLD OF YOURSELF

As with every other attainment in the Christian life, prayerful praying is not automatic. Paul urges Timothy, "Exercise thyself rather unto godliness.... Fight the good fight of faith, lay hold on eternal life" (1 Tim. 4:7; 6:12). I thus plead with you to seek a more fervent and faithful prayer life, with effort, urgency, and dependence on Christ and the Holy Spirit. You must practice the discipline of self-control, which is not a natural ability but a fruit of the Spirit purchased by Jesus Christ at the cross (Gal. 5:22–24).

Beware of the trap of thinking that some people are more prayerful and holy by nature, and you just aren't one of them. The halo we set on the heads of others may be an excuse for our own laziness. J. C. Ryle asked, "What is the reason that some believers are so much brighter and holier than others?" Out of years of experience, Ryle answered,

> I believe that those who are not eminently holy pray little.... When a man is once converted, his progress in holiness will be much in accordance with his own diligence in the use of God's appointed means. And I confidently assert that the principal means by which most believers have become great in the Church of Christ is the habit of diligent private prayer.[10]

10. J. C. Ryle, *A Call to Prayer* (Moscow, Idaho: Charles Nolan Publishers, 2000), 13–15.

Let me give you some important principles of how to take hold of yourself for prayer.

Remember the Value of Prayer
The disciples wanted to learn to pray because they saw the place that prayer had in the life of our Lord (Luke 11:1). We should always remember these five truths: (1) prayer is essential for the well-being of your own soul; (2) prayer is essential for you to fulfill your calling in your family, church, and nation; (3) prayer is one of the most Christlike activities you can engage in; (4) prayer is God's appointed means of distributing the blessings of His kingdom and the gifts of Christ to His people; (5) and unoffered prayer, not unanswered prayer, is our greatest problem—for they who ask not, have not (James 4:2).

We must value praying, however, even when we do not see answers. It can be God's mercy to deny us answered prayer in order to foster growth in believing submission to Him. Faith's roots often grow deepest in the soil of unanswered prayer. William Carey labored as a missionary in India for eight years before baptizing the first convert from Hinduism to Christ.[11] Yet in those years Carey learned to live for the glory of God alone. He wrote, "I feel that it is good to commit my soul, my body, and my all, into the hands of God. Then the world appears little, the

---

11. Timothy George, *Faithful Witness: The Life and Mission of William Carey* (Birmingham, Ala.: New Hope, 1991), 131.

promises great, and God an all-sufficient portion."[12] God's delay became marrow for Carey's soul. That still happens today to believers when, exercised in prayer by God's silences, they find more of God Himself. God is always greater and more valuable than His answers. The greatest mercy is to find God, not His mercies. Then we discover that when we ask for silver, God may wrap His silences in gold that doesn't perish! William Bridge said, "A praying man can never be very miserable, whatever his condition be, for he has the ear of God.... It is a mercy to pray, even though I never receive the mercy prayed for."[13]

If unanswered prayer can be valuable, how much more valuable answered prayer can be! The Lord Jesus Christ has told us that a life of asking, seeking, and knocking is a life of receiving, finding, and opening doors to us (Matt. 7:7). God has a way of either answering our prayer or giving us something even better—that is, what we should have been asking for in the first place. Never underestimate the importance of prayer. Referring to events recorded in Acts 12:1–10, Thomas Watson said, "The angel fetched Peter out of prison, but it was prayer that fetched the angel."[14] I once visited a woman

12. As quoted in George, *Faithful Witness*, 104.

13. William Bridge, *A Lifting Up for the Downcast* (Edinburgh: Banner of Truth, 1990), 55.

14. Thomas Watson, *A Divine Cordial* (Wilmington, Del.: Sovereign Grace Publishers, 1972), 18.

who was ill, and after praying for her physical needs and for her soul, I apologized for not being able to do anything more. She wisely rebuked me, saying, "Pastor, you've done something more important for me than the physicians—you've prayed for me!"

Pray, persevere in praying, and do not grow weary or faint (Luke 18:1). Remember that in the waiting time between sowing and reaping, plants are growing. Keep watering them with your prayers.

Maintain the Priority of Prayer
Many activities have their special times and seasons (Eccl. 3:1–8), but prayer is an activity for all seasons (1 Thess. 5:17). Our Lord devoted Himself to prayer (Luke 5:16). In His humanity, He grew weary from His labors, but He rose early to pray in solitude even after a busy night's work (Mark 1:35). Sometimes He prayed through the night (Luke 6:12). If the incarnate Son of God needed to pray often to His heavenly Father, then how much more do we need to make prayer a priority in our lives? The Lord warns us, "Without me ye can do nothing" (John 15:5). Prayer is the greatest part of our spiritual warfare (Eph. 6:18). John Bunyan stressed the priority of prayer by asserting that we can do more than pray after we have prayed, but we cannot do more than pray until we have prayed. He then concluded: "Pray often, for

prayer is a shield to the soul, a sacrifice to God, and a scourge for Satan."[15]

To prioritize is to rank some things higher than others. Is it possible that your prayer life suffers because something else ranks too high with you? Does your social life crowd out prayer? Is the use of electronic media such as the Internet, television, or radio hindering your prayers? Media may do so by absorbing too much precious time while your prayer life languishes. Or media might hinder your prayers by filling your mind with worldly thoughts and occupations so that your prayers become shallow, cold, self-centered, materialistic, or unmotivated—and thus infrequent. Prioritizing prayer will require putting other activities in a lower place in order to make room for communion with God.

Even if your prayers seem lifeless, do not stop praying. For the moment, dullness may seem hard to overcome, but refusing to pray at all is the fruit of presumption, self-sufficiency, and slothfulness. When the outward form of prayer is gone, all is gone. It is easy to pray when you feel like a sailboat gliding forward in a favoring wind. But you should also pray when you must like an icebreaker smash your way through an arctic sea one foot at a time. No matter what, make prayer your personal spiritual priority.

---

15. *The Works of John Bunyan*, ed. George Offor (1854; repr., Edinburgh: Banner of Truth, 1991), 1:65.

Speak with Sincerity in Prayer

Psalm 62:8 says, "Trust in him at all times; ye people, pour out your heart before him: God is a refuge for us." To pray with your mouth what is not truly in your heart is hypocrisy (Isa. 29:13)—unless you are confessing the coldness of your heart and crying out for heartwarming grace. Sincere prayers can take many forms. Sometimes a sincere prayer such as Psalm 119 is long and carefully crafted. Sometimes a sincere prayer such as Psalm 86:11b is quite simple: "Unite my heart to fear thy name." Or consider Luke 18:13: "God be merciful to me a sinner." Either way, settle for nothing less than sincerity in your prayer.

Sincerity in prayer requires integrity in all of our relationships. For example, consider the relationship of husbands to their wives. First Peter 3:7 says, "Likewise, ye husbands, dwell with them according to knowledge, giving honour unto the wife, as unto the weaker vessel, and as being heirs together of the grace of life; that your prayers be not hindered." Taking hold of yourself in prayer may require taking hold of your bad attitude or mistreatment of your wife, if that is the case. When your wife hears you pray, does her heart say, "Amen!" or "Hypocrite!"? Perhaps the first prayer you need to pray is a prayer of repentance for not showing compassion and honor to your helpmeet.

Heartfelt sincerity in prayer is paramount to God. Be encouraged to strive for sincerity in prayer by these words of Thomas Brooks:

> God looks not at the elegancy of your prayers, to
> see how neat they are; nor yet at the geometry of
> your prayers to see how long they are; nor yet at
> the arithmetic of your prayers, to see how many
> they are; nor yet at the music of your prayers, nor
> yet at the sweetness of your voice, nor yet at the
> logic of your prayers; but at the sincerity of your
> prayers, how hearty they are. There is no prayer
> acknowledged, approved, accepted, recorded, or
> rewarded by God, but that wherein the heart is
> sincerely and wholly. The true mother would not
> have the child divided. As God loves a broken and
> a contrite heart, so he loathes a divided heart.[16]

Sincere prayer takes every part of our being to perform. Not merely the heart but also the mind, the will, the emotions, and even the body must all be turned to God in a real and intimate way. Sincere prayer does not close its eyes in mere formality. It instead opens the eyes of the soul to behold the panoramic view of God's glory and His promises recorded in Scripture.

Cultivate Continual Prayer

"Pray without ceasing," says Paul in 1 Thessalonians 5:17. Whatever our calling or trade, prayer must be our work throughout the day (Rom. 12:12; Col. 4:2). We fulfill this mandate in a number of ways. First, we maintain an attitude of prayer throughout the day. As one man said, when we finish talking to

---

16. *Works of Thomas Brooks*, 2:256–57.

God, we don't "hang up"—we keep the line open. We live moment by moment in the presence of God and should be conscious of it. Spurgeon quoted Alleine as writing, "Though I am apt to be unsettled and quickly set off the hinges, yet, methinks, I am like a bird out of the nest. I am never quiet till I am in my old way of communion with God; like the needle in the compass, that is restless till it be turned to the pole."[17]

Second, to pray without ceasing we should establish set times of prayer in our daily schedule. We should not start our day's work without a time of private prayer, and before we fall asleep we should speak with our God. Meals are appropriate times to pause, give thanks, and lift up our needs. There may be other times in your schedule or times when you are with people you regularly see that you can turn into opportunities for prayer, especially the daily practice of family worship.

Third, saturate the routines of your earthly life with meditation on the relationship of things earthly and temporal to things heavenly and eternal. Be like the young woman who, as she dressed in the morning, prayed for God to clothe her with Christ; as she cleaned the house, prayed for God to wash sin from her family's lives; and as she cooked supper, prayed

---

17. Charles H. Spurgeon, *Lectures to My Students* (London: Passmore and Alabaster, 1875), 1:41.

for God to help the preacher to prepare spiritual food for his flock.

Fourth, we should be alert and ready to pray at a moment's notice. Maintain a state of spiritual alertness (Eph. 6:18; Col. 4:2) like the soldier in the squad who carries the radio and is always ready to call in support. Whenever you feel the least impulse to pray or see a need to pray, do so. Even if you are in the midst of a difficult job that demands concentration, always obey the impulse to prayer—in a manner that is safe and wise. The impulse may be a groaning of the Spirit, and we must never regard the Spirit's promptings as an intrusion. Do not tell yourself to wait until it is more convenient; start praying immediately. Learn to pray inwardly while the outward man is busy with daily tasks.

Organize for Prayer

Paul modeled regular intercession for a number of different churches and Christians, including some he had never met (Col. 1:9; 2:1). He commanded Christians to offer "supplication for all saints" (Eph. 6:18) and for "all men" (1 Tim. 2:1), but if we don't have a system for our intercession, we will hardly pray for anyone on a regular basis.

Organize your petitions by some system or list. It may not seem very spiritual to use a prayer list, but it is eminently practical. I encourage you to develop lists for your personal prayers and for your family worship. You might divide a list into different categories, such as petitions for every day, every week, and every month. Periodically update your list or refresh your system. Use resources such as your church directory, dividing the names into manageable groups that you can pray for at one time. Be reasonable and do not overburden yourself, but discipline yourself to pray much for many people.

Find ways to pray intelligently for missions. Regularly read newsletters and updates from churches and missionaries, and pray for them immediately—or you might forget. Use books and websites such as *Operation World* and *Voice of the Martyrs*. Buy a map of the world or an area of special concern for you, and mark it up as you pray for the work of the gospel among the nations.

Stay focused in all your intercessory praying. Be specific in your prayers, be earnest while you pray, be expectant that your prayers will be answered, and be patient in waiting for divine fruit. If you pray this way, intercessory praying may become your most fruitful and valuable ministry.

Use the Bible as Your Guide for Prayer

One reason your prayer life may be drooping is that you have neglected the Holy Scriptures. The Westminster divines held that "the whole word of God is of use to direct us in the duty of prayer" (Larger Catechism, Q. 186). Prayer is a two-way conversation. We need to listen to God, not just talk to Him. We do not listen to God by emptying our minds and waiting for a thought to spontaneously come to mind. That can easily turn into non-Christian mysticism. We listen to God by filling our minds with the Bible because the Bible is God speaking in written form (Ps. 1:2).

Our Lord Jesus Christ says in John 15:7, "If ye abide in me, and my words abide in you, ye shall ask what ye will, and it shall be done unto you." Therefore, the Word is essential to a life of answered prayer. Later in this booklet, I will talk about using God's promises for prayer. Here I want to draw attention to praying with a mind shaped by the truths and words of Scripture.

When you read the prayers of godly men and women of the past, it is impressive how the Word of God filled their prayers. In the house churches in China in the twentieth century, many Christians had no Bible, but they had memorized long portions of Scripture. Their prayers were full of Scripture, and they sometimes even recited their entire theology in the presence of God.[18]

One benefit of praying from a heart soaked in Scripture is that your prayers will increasingly reflect the heart of God. Though the Bible encourages us to pray for our physical needs and afflictions, it places the emphasis upon God's spiritual kingdom—as the order of the Lord's Prayer shows. Paul's prayers for the churches reflect a heart captivated by a love for

---

18. David Wang, "Lessons from the Prayer Habits of the Church in China," in *Teach Us to Pray*, 251.

holiness and a mind set on the glory of Christ. The apostle consistently prayed for the church to grow in wisdom, love, hope, and good works.[19] His prayer requests show a soul aflame with desire for the gospel to save lost sinners. Praying with an open Bible will make your prayers more obedient to Christ's command, "Seek ye first the kingdom of God" (Matt. 6:33).

Refresh Your Prayers with Biblical Variety
Another benefit of Bible study for prayer is that the Word of God keeps our prayers from falling into ruts carved by our personalities. The Scriptures present various kinds of prayer: praise of God's glories, confession of our sins, petition for our needs (spiritual and physical), thanks for God's mercies, intercession for others (family, friends, church, nation, and the world), and our affirmation that we are confident that God is willing and able to answer what we have prayed. We have a tendency to favor some kinds of prayer to the neglect of others.

For example, one person might gravitate toward intercession but neglect thanksgiving. Paul says in Philippians 4:6, "Be careful [or anxious] for nothing, but in every thing by prayer and supplication with thanksgiving let your requests be made known unto

---

19. For example, consider Ephesians 1:15–19; 3:14–21; Philippians 1:9–11; and Colossians 1:9–12. See Donald A. Carson, *Praying with Paul: A Call for Spiritual Reformation* (Grand Rapids: Baker Academic, 2014).

God." Another person might delight in praising God but shy away from confessing sin, forgetting that the apostle John tells us that one mark of walking in the light of God is confession of sins and finding forgiveness from God through the blood of His Son (1 John 1:7–9). Periodically examine your prayers to see if they are out of balance, and give more attention to the kinds of prayer you are neglecting.

Take hold of yourself for prayer. Exercise self-discipline in your thinking and pursue a life of prayer. Remind yourself of how important prayer is, make it a high priority, avoid dead formality, and always be conscious that you live in the presence of God. Organize your life and use your Bible for the sake of prayer. Do not wait for God to strike you with a spiritual lightning bolt to refresh your prayer life. At the very least, put up a lightning rod!

TAKE HOLD OF GOD

Deep within us, we know that it is impossible to overcome prayerlessness by our own strength. The sacredness, gift, and power of prayer are far above human means. God's grace is necessary for prayerful praying. Yet grace does not make us passively wait for God to give it. Grace moves us to seek the Lord. David sings in Psalm 25:1, "Unto thee, O LORD, do I lift up my soul" (see also Pss. 86:4; 143:8). Paul commands us in Colossians 3:1–2, "If ye then be risen with Christ, seek those things which are above, where Christ sitteth on the right hand of God. Set your affection on things above, not on things on the earth." So direct your mind and affections toward our covenant God in Christ, and draw near to His throne of grace.

Just as Jacob wrestled with the Angel of the Lord and would not let Him go until He blessed him, so we must take hold of God until He blesses us. The prophet Isaiah lamented the prayerlessness of his own generation: "There is none that calleth upon thy name, that stirreth up himself to take hold of thee" (Isa. 64:7). Will you stir yourself up to take hold of God? Allow me to give you several practical ways to do this by God's grace.

Exercise Faith in Jesus Christ for Prayer
How can sinners take hold of God except in Jesus Christ? Hebrews 10:19–22 tells us that it is only by His blood and intercession as our high priest that we can boldly "enter into the holiest," that is, the place where God dwells on high. Therefore all our prayers must be offered by faith in Christ. Through Him we have access to the Father, for Christ alone is the Mediator between God and men (Eph. 2:18; 1 Tim. 2:5).

George Downame said that we must ask "how it cometh to pass that man being stained and polluted with sin, and by reason thereof an enemy of God, should have any access to God, or be admitted to any speech with him, who is most just and terrible, a consuming fire, and hating all iniquity with perfect hatred." Downame answers his own question:

"Therefore of necessity a mediator was to come between God and man, who reconciling us unto God, and covering our imperfections, might make both our persons and our prayers acceptable under God."[20]

This state of affairs illuminates what the Lord Jesus meant when He taught us to pray *in His name* (John 14:13–14; 15:16; 16:23–24, 26). We dare not go to God on the basis of who we are or what we have done, but only on the basis of Christ and His finished work. The more you learn to pray with a mind set upon Christ as our Great High Priest, the more you will be able to take hold of God and pray with the boldness of true faith.

Plead God's Promises in Prayer

In His sovereignty, God has bound Himself by the promises He makes to us in His Word. Turn His promises into prayer and claim them as your own. Let the rich substance of God's promises be the primary substance of your prayers. Psalm 119:25 says, "My soul cleaveth unto the dust: quicken thou me according to thy word." Thomas Manton wrote, "One good way to get comfort is to plead the promise of God in prayer.... Show him his handwriting; God is tender of his word."[21]

---

20. George Downame, *A Godly and Learned Treatise of Prayer* (Cambridge: by Roger Daniel for Nicolas Bourn, 1640), 68.

21. *The Complete Works of Thomas Manton* (London: James Nisbet, 1872), 6:242.

Some years ago, an elderly friend brought me a spiritual letter from my father, who died while leading a church service and passed straight from the pulpit to glory in 1993. My father wrote the letter in the 1950s, shortly after his conversion. "I thought you might like to have this," the friend said. "Like to?" I said, "I would *love* to have this." I sat down and read it immediately with great pleasure—it was so personal not only because of its rich personal content but also because it was in my father's handwriting. How do you think your Father in heaven feels when you show Him His own handwriting in prayer by quoting His own Word back to Him, pleading the promises it contains?

Pray God's promises back to Him. John Trapp wrote, "Promises must be prayed over. God loves to be burdened with, and to be importuned [urgently pressed with requests] in his own words; to be sued upon his own bond. Prayer is a putting God's promises into suit. And it is no arrogancy nor presumption, to burden God, as it were, with his promise.... Such prayers will be nigh the Lord day and night (1 Kings 8:59); he can as little deny them, as deny himself."[22]

Likewise, William Gurnall wrote, "Prayer is nothing but the promise reversed, or God's Word formed into an argument, and retorted by faith upon God

---

22. John Trapp, *A Commentary on the Old and New Testaments*, ed. W. Hugh Martin (London: Richard D. Dickinson, 1867), 1:121 (on Gen. 32:9).

again."[23] And what is the greatest promise of the
Word and the sum of all promises but the gospel of
Christ crucified for our sins? So pray in the name
of Christ, pleading God's promises, knowing that
"all the promises of God in him are yea, and in him
Amen, unto the glory of God" (2 Cor. 1:20).

Look to the Glorious Trinity in Prayer
Much prayerlessness in our prayers is due to our
thoughtlessness toward God. Our prayers may be
prompted by the stress of an immediate need or
crisis, or they may become mere habitual talking to
ourselves. But God dwells in our prayers most when
our minds most dwell on Him. Therefore, when you
pray, meditate on how the gospel reveals the Father,
the Son, and the Holy Spirit to draw sinners to God.
Before rushing into your list of requests, bring to
mind Scripture texts that speak of the glory and
goodness of our God, and turn those texts into praise.

Ephesians 2:18 tells us how the three persons of
the Trinity operate in our worship and prayers: "For
through him [Christ Jesus] we both have access by
one Spirit unto the Father." Prayer is like a golden
chain that runs from the Father through the Son and
in the Spirit back to the Father again. Prayer is commanded by the Father, made acceptable by the Son,
shaped into desires and words by the Spirit, and sent

---

23. William Gurnall, *The Christian in Complete Armour* (1662–1665;
repr., Edinburgh: Banner of Truth, 2002), 2:88.

back up to the Son, who, through His intercession, presents it as acceptable and well pleasing to His heavenly Father. So lean heavily on the Spirit to help you compose your prayers, trust in Christ to make your prayers effectual, and rest in the Father's love that sent both Son and Spirit down from heaven. Through the Son and in the Spirit, your prayers will reach the ears of the Father on high.

John Owen advises us to commune with each person of the triune God in our prayers.[24] He did so based on Paul's benediction recorded in 2 Corinthians 13:14: "The grace of the Lord Jesus Christ, and the love of God, and the communion of the Holy Ghost, be with you all. Amen." So in your prayer life, pursue a deeper and more experiential knowledge of

- the riches of grace in Christ's person and work,
- the glory of the electing and adopting love of the Father, and
- the comfort of fellowship with God by the indwelling Holy Spirit.

In this way, you will pray not just for God's benefits but for God Himself, which will serve as a blessing both for you and for your church. Your

---

24. *The Works of John Owen* (1850–1853; repr., Edinburgh: Banner of Truth, 1965–1968), 2:1–274. This excellent book has also been published as John Owen, *Communion with the Triune God*, ed. Kelly M. Kapic and Justin Taylor (Wheaton, Ill.: Crossway, 2007).

sense of God-intimacy and God-dependency experientially known in private will spill over into your public life so that you will also, by the Spirit's grace, encourage other people to depend on God and seek intimate communion with Him.

Believe That God Hears and Answers Prayer

I fear that we often do not believe that God hears our prayers—as is evident by our surprise when answers come. If we do not trust that God answers prayer, we call into question His fatherly love toward us. Since He is our God and Father only for the sake of Christ His Son, lack of confidence in the prayer-hearing Father boils down to mistrust in the finished work of Christ.

Hebrews 4:14–16 says,

> Seeing then that we have a great high priest, that is passed into the heavens, Jesus the Son of God, let us hold fast our profession. For we have not an high priest which cannot be touched with the feeling of our infirmities; but was in all points tempted like as we are, yet without sin. Let us therefore come boldly unto the throne of grace, that we may obtain mercy, and find grace to help in time of need.

Let us then pray with confidence that our Father's heart is full of grace because our Savior's hands were pierced for us. Let us not be unbelieving, but believing in our prayers. Let us go to God, day and night, remembering that He doesn't punch a clock when He is available, for He doesn't post visiting hours. His ear is always attuned to His people's cries and sighs, petitions and confessions, praises and thanksgivings.

What an open, generous heart God the Father has toward His children! It was He who predestined us to adoption as His children and heirs (Eph. 1:3–5). It was He who sent His Son to die for our sins (Eph. 1:7). It was He who has sent His Spirit into our hearts so that we would cry to Him, "Abba, Father" (Gal. 4:6). Child of God, do not fear to come home to your Father in heaven. Though you may have backslidden in your prayers, if you seek Him He will run to meet you. He will embrace you. He will kiss you with the blessings of His Spirit. Get up out of your prayerlessness and run to the Father! The blood of Christ will cleanse you from all sin. The Spirit of Christ will stir up renewed desires to pray and to seek God's face (Ps. 27:8).

Seek the Glory of God in Prayer
Jesus Christ taught us to pray to the Father, "Hallowed be thy name" (Matt. 6:9), and He Himself prayed, "Father, glorify thy name" (John 12:28). James Fisher explains that God's name includes "everything by which he is pleased to make himself known," including His names, titles, attributes, ordinances, word, and works.[25] A good name is "the

---

25. James Fisher, *The Assembly's Shorter Catechism Explained* (Stoke-on-Trent, U.K.: Berith Publications, 1998), 272; cf. Westminster Shorter Catechism, Q. 54.

having of reputation and esteem, especially among the sober and religious (Pss. 16:3; 101:6)."[26] Just as a man should be zealous to maintain a good name in the community, God acts to exalt His own reputation in the eyes of the world.

A profound sense of God's glorious majesty and holiness must fill us at the very beginning of prayer. It is vital to extol God's glory in all our prayers. I was deeply impressed on a trip to Northern Ireland with the prayers of several Christians I met there. The first half of their prayers was often devoted to recounting the attributes of God and praising Him as Creator, Provider, and Redeemer. They were God-centered prayers, praising Him and worshiping Him just as David does in Psalm 145.

What does it mean to pray for God's name to be hallowed? It means to pray that God would cause all His creatures to acknowledge Him as God and to honor Him as holy. The Heidelberg Catechism says that this petition means,

> Grant us, first, rightly to know Thee (John 17:3; Matt. 16:17; James 1:5; Ps. 119:105), and to hallow, magnify, and praise Thee in all Thy works, in which Thy power, goodness, justice, mercy, and truth shine forth (Ps. 119:137; Rom. 11:33–36); and further, that we so order our whole life, our thoughts, words and deeds, that Thy name may

---

26. Fisher, *Shorter Catechism Explained*, 336; cf. Westminster Shorter Catechism, Q. 77.

not be blasphemed, but honored and praised on our account (Ps. 71:8).[27]

To hallow God's name, people must know who He is. Yet bare knowledge does not move sinners to honor God (Rom. 1:21); we need a heart knowledge that moves us to worship God in spirit and in truth (John 4:24)—that is, with our spirits moved by the truth of God's Word, illuminated by His Spirit. Knowing, fearing, and loving His holiness will then lead us to honor Him with the holiness of obedience. We must pray for God to be honored in us by the powerful, inward operation of His grace.

For example, you might pray, "Lord, my son is unsaved. Remove the darkness from his eyes, let the glory of Jesus Christ shine into his mind, and enable him to repent and believe. Open his heart so that he worships Thee with the love Thou dost so richly deserve. Fill his life with holiness for Thy own glory." When you pray that prayer, you are praying that the name of God will be made to appear great in the world. If your son believes, the fame and reputation of our God will be increased. This should be the heartbeat of all our prayers.

Develop a Right Heart toward God in Prayer
When God hears our prayers, He looks into our hearts. Solomon prayed, "What prayer and

---

27. Heidelberg Catechism, Q. 122, in Dennison, *Reformed Confessions*, 2:798.

supplication soever be made by any man... hear thou in heaven thy dwelling place, and forgive, and do, and give to every man according to his ways, whose heart thou knowest (for thou, even thou only, knowest the hearts of all the children of men)" (1 Kings 8:38–39). God's ears are open to our prayers when His eyes see the righteous motives of our hearts (Ps. 66:18–20). John Calvin wrote, "Now for framing prayer duly and properly, let this be the first rule: that we be disposed in mind and heart as befits those who enter conversation with God."[28]

The heart is crucial in prayer. Brooks wrote,

> Prayer is only lovely and weighty, as the heart is in it, and not otherwise. It is not the lifting up of the voice, nor the wringing of the hands, nor the beating of the breasts, nor an affected tone, nor studied motions, nor seraphical expressions, but the stirrings of the heart, that God looks at in prayer. God hears no more than the heart speaks.[29]

Just as our persons must be clothed in the righteousness of Christ, our prayers must be driven by attitudes formed in us by the Spirit of Christ if we would have God accept them. The more this is so, the more our prayers will take hold of God and please Him. This includes a heart of

28. Calvin, *Institutes*, 3.20.4.

29. *Works of Thomas Brooks*, 2:257.

- faith toward God: "What things soever ye desire, when ye pray, believe that ye receive them, and ye shall have them" (Mark 11:24).

- repentance from sin: "If I regard iniquity in my heart, the Lord will not hear me" (Ps. 66:18).

- fervent, holy desire: "The effectual fervent prayer of a righteous man availeth much" (James 5:16).

- humility before God: "God be merciful to me a sinner" (Luke 18:13).

- boldness in Christ: "Let us therefore come boldly unto the throne of grace, that we may obtain mercy, and find grace to help in time of need" (Heb. 4:16).

- love and forgiveness for other people: "And when ye stand praying, forgive, if ye have ought against any: that your Father also which is in heaven may forgive you your trespasses" (Mark 11:25).

- thankfulness: "In every thing by prayer and supplication with thanksgiving let your requests be made known unto God" (Phil. 4:6).

All in all, we should pray with a childlike heart toward "our Father which art in heaven." Manton said, "A word from a child moves the father more than an orator can move all his hearers."[30] Simple trust, reverence, and love please God. To come as a child to the Father is to honor Him in the highest degree and to engage His deepest compassion.

Rest with Contentment in God's All-Sufficiency in Prayer
Christ comforted His disciples with the words, "Fear not, little flock; for it is your Father's good pleasure to give you the kingdom" (Luke 12:32). Sometimes the greatest answer to prayer is the peace of God—that is, the presence of the God of peace (Phil. 4:6–7, 9). This gives contentment, for then we have Christ, who is life itself (Phil. 1:21).

Unanswered prayers are sometimes God's instrument to uncover desires in us that have grown too big and too worldly (James 4:3–4). Covetousness makes sinful demands of God (Ps. 78:18–19). But godliness with contentment is great gain (1 Tim. 6:6). Divine contentment takes our eyes off worldly things and lifts them to the source of happiness and fulfillment. That does not mean all of our personal desires will be met, nor will it sweep us up to heaven in outward luxury and ease. The secret of contentment, says Paul, is that it carries a believer through thick and thin, plenty and want, sickness and health (Phil. 4:11–13). This kind of contentment can only be realized by taking hold of God through prayer and waiting on Him for continual supplies of His grace.

---

30. *Works of Thomas Manton*, 1:28.

Contentment does not cause us to cease praying for deliverance from evil and asking for enjoyment of good, but it comes with a humbling sense that God is all we truly need (Psalm 131). Even if everything goes wrong, we can still rejoice in our God and Savior (Hab. 3:17–19). This is the ultimate sense of what it means to take hold of God in prayer: to take Him as your portion forever (Ps. 73:25–26). Then God becomes not only the One who answers prayer but also the ultimate answer to our prayers.

Then our Father's will becomes more important than our own, and, like Jacob, we experience that precisely when we surrender to God, when we lay hold of Him in victorious contentment and submission. Only then do we understand that all true prayer is grounded in Jesus' great petition, "Thy will be done." Our prayer then is not that God will bend His will to ours but ours to His, so that we may think, speak, do, and wait upon His will in every situation. As Isaac Watts said,

> Father, I wait thy daily will;
> Thou shalt divide my portion still;
> Grant me on earth what seems thee best,
> Till death and heav'n reveal the rest.[31]

That is what it means to take hold of God.

---

31. *The Psalms and Hymns of Isaac Watts,* hymn 43, part 2, Christian Classics Ethereal Library, http://www.ccel.org/ccel/watts/psalmshymns.html.

CONCLUSION

Prayer is difficult and demanding work. Sometimes we get on our knees but find ourselves spiritually dry; it is hard to get water out of a dry sponge. When we rise from our knees, we realize we haven't truly prayed in our prayer. We must fall back on our knees again, praying to pray. At other times, prayer is amazing, glorious, delightful work. On still other occasions, we feel like Hannah, pouring out our soul with complaints and grief before God in great distress (1 Sam. 1:10–17). I suppose that there is scarcely a believer on earth who cannot identify with these extremes. Prayerful prayer will sometimes lead you to profound sadness as you see yourself in your wretched sinfulness, but it will also lead you to profound joy when you "know the love of Christ, which passeth knowledge" and are "filled with all the fulness of God" (Eph. 3:19).

In this booklet I have set forth high ideals for the pursuit of a richer prayer life. However, my aim is not to discourage you but to encourage you. Learning truly to pray in our prayers is not just a matter of making a decision to work harder or to find a new method. It involves trials, warfare, the enabling Spirit of God, and a growing realization that our prayers depend on the merits of Christ, not on the intensity of our feelings. It is a process of growth inseparable from our sanctification, and thus unending until we reach glory.

Ask God to make you a praying Elijah who knows what it means to battle unbelief and despair, even as you strive to grow in prayer and grateful communion with God. Isn't it interesting that James presents Elijah in James 5:17 as a person of "passions," as someone quite like you and me? He prayed in his praying, but he could also despair in his despairing (1 Kings 19). When you hit low spots in your spiritual life, remember the tenderness of God toward Elijah. Sometimes the answer to depression, as it was for the prophet, is not more effort but a good meal and a night's sleep so that you can resume the battle tomorrow.

The point is to press on by faith in Jesus Christ. If you have fallen, get up. If you stand, beware lest you fall. No matter where you are in your spiritual journey, the greatest danger is to get distracted, to stop where you are and become complacent and negligent in prayer.[32]

A couple stopped to help a man pacing back and forth in front of his Cadillac, which was parked at the side of a road. He explained, "I left home in a hurry to get to an important meeting, but I ran out of gas." The couple had a small can of gas in their trunk, so they poured it into the Cadillac and told the owner,

---

32. For more meditations on how to strengthen your prayer life, see James W. Beeke and Joel R. Beeke, *Developing a Healthy Prayer Life: 31 Meditations on Communing with God* (Grand Rapids: Reformation Heritage Books, 2010).

"There is a service station just down the road; make sure you stop to get more gas." The man sped away, profusely grateful. Ten miles later the couple saw the same Cadillac on the roadside, the owner pacing beside it even more frantically. He was in such a hurry that he failed to stop at the service station.

How could this man be so foolish? But isn't this precisely what we are prone to do with our spiritual lives? We are so busy pressing on to the next meeting, the next activity, the next item on our list, that we fail to take time to refuel our lives with prayer, and soon our spiritual tank is empty and we are stranded on the side of the road to the celestial city.[33]

Persevere in private prayer no matter how busy you are or how listless you feel. Entertain no excuses for ceasing to pray.

Remember, you and I absolutely need private prayer not just to bring our needs to God but because private prayer is an essential part of our worship. Prayer is not just self-talk, quiet meditation, or coming to God with a shopping list; it is coming humbly in faith to God, desiring to commune with Him—to have serious conversation with the God of the universe. We do not pray to change God but so that He might change us, making us more worshipful.

Press on in your prayers toward the mark for the prize of the high calling of God in Christ Jesus.

---

33. I am indebted to my colleague David VanBrugge for this illustration from a sermon he preached on January 3, 2016.

Since prayer in its essence is communion with God, there are riches you have not yet discovered, depths you have not reached, and joys that yet await you— all in and through Christ by the Holy Spirit. What a blessing it is to pray! Prayer is nothing less than a journey into the heart of the Father, following the way opened up by the Son, under the guidance of the Word and Spirit of God.